G E M S T O N E S
A N D
C O L O R

(and a whole lot more)

FOR BETTER HEALTH
HEALING
HAPPINESS

MARIE WILLIAMS CORNELIO

1985

 PUBLISHING COMPANY

P.O. BOX 7-966

West Hartford, Connecticut

PRINTING HISTORY

1st Printing ..... February 1986
2nd Printing ..... September 1986

ISBN: 0-936703-00-8

Library of Congress Card Catalog

Number: 85-052327

D E D I C A T I O N

To Marty

For love, support –
And stoic patience.

SPECIAL THANKS

Julie Nichols

Beverly R. Titus
Gemini Word Pro

ARTWORK

Bob Gorske
Kyle Niles

A C K N O W L E D G E M E N T S

With love and gratitude

To my mentors,

Marjorie Buckley Turcotte

And

Matthew McDonnell

Without whom –

This book could not have been written.

TABLE OF CONTENTS

Have fun with this book. It can help to bring more joy into your life because you'll learn to flow, be more serene. The more love and happiness you can give to yourself, the more you'll have to give. When you're content, it's infectious - you make others feel good too.

You see, one person <u>can</u> make a difference!

M.W.C.

INTRODUCTION

We firmly believe that there is nothing upon this earth that was not placed here for a reason. Ecology has taught us of the fine balance of nature. Each insect, each plant, each animal serves its purpose.

So it is with gemstones. If they served no purpose, there would be only one gemstone, just as there would be one tree, one color, on this planet. Yet the variety is endless. Like us, each is unique and has its own purpose.

How wonderful that we can again tap into this information, for the spiritual value of gems was known to the Ancient Ones.

Breastplates, worn by powerful rulers, were adorned with lapis, topaz, opal, emerald, ruby, white sapphire (now called diamond), jade in various colors, garnet, alexandrite and amethyst plus many more. Jewels accompanied departed souls on their last journey. Today, there are those who still wear amulets (an ornament worn as a charm against evil or to bring good fortune.) Just as the cross has become symbolic of Christianity (yet it is an ancient symbol), and the sacred Egyptian emblem, the ankh, (a cross with a ring at the top) is symbolic of life, *gemstones are an integral part of mankind's history.*

Everything has energy. Man, animals, plants, and stones have it. It is the sun that replenishes us, restores our vitality, nourishes our plant life. The night is soft and mellow; the sun, bright and dazzling; and water is the great purifier.

We will work with these forces of nature with our gemstones.

CHAPTER I

HOW GEMSTONES WORK

AND WHY

HOW GEMSTONES WORK AND WHY

Everything has a vibration - everything. You can't see or touch it, but you know it's there. It's instinctively or intuitively sensed.

You see someone and you <u>know</u> you'd like them. You've not even spoken to them. Intuitively, you "felt" their vibration. Yet other people can make you uncomfortable because you know instinctively that your vibrations do not blend. Or you go to a party and, on entering the front door, you <u>know</u> this is going to be one of the best parties ever. But how did you know? You felt it.

The animal kingdom lives by its instincts. We have the same capability, but we generally ignore our intuitive senses. We're changing that. We're developing an awareness we've not had for a long, long time.

You have a favorite color and wear it often because it makes you feel good. Why? Because it too has a vibration, an energy, that you are instinctively drawn to. Each color gives something, does something for you. But until now, you may not have been aware of it.

A natural fabric, such as cotton, wool, or flannel, has a stronger vibration than a synthetic or one that has a synthetic added (95% cotton, 5% synthetic.) This does not imply that it has a better vibration, just a stronger one.

A natural stone, as opposed to one that is dyed, also has a stronger vibration. The onyx group would be a good example of this.

You are a planet unto yourself and contain all the minerals of the earth within you, and perhaps there's an imbalance. Different stones can begin to work with that imbalance. After all, they have the minerals of the earth within them because that's what created the colorations of the stones.

If all this seems a little far-fetched, remember it was the ruby that enabled the laser to work; now a crystal can be used as well.

Any time you identify with a stone or color, and what it can do for you, that in itself is a building process and what you're building is a more balanced, happier you. The cells of your body will attune and respond to it.

Understand that the stones and colors cannot do it alone. When you decide to become more balanced, happier, more flowing, the stones and colors will enhance it.

At the <u>very moment</u> you decide to wear a stone for its attributes, you open a door for yourself. You make the decision and the action is put into motion.

There is no good luck or success stone. Too bad. But like the old "lucky" rabbit's foot (not so lucky for the rabbit), if you believe something will bring you good fortune, it will. If you believe that placing an amethyst under your pillow will intensify your dreams and your recall of them, it will. Your belief makes it so. (Actually an azurite works best for dreams.) But it's really not that important. Your belief is.

We'd like to define some of the terms we will be using, such as "flowing", "spiritual", "energies going inward or outward".

Perhaps the best definition of

"flowing" would be: to allow. To allow others to be who and what they are. To accept them as themselves, not the image we feel they should be. They have that right, just as you do. Accept the things that you absolutely cannot change. Suppose for weeks now you've planned an outdoor barbecue and as your guests arrive, there's an extremely violent thunderstorm. How will you react? Inwardly, you're seething with frustration. What are you going to do about it? You can get angry, tear your hair out, jump up and down, but - look out the window, the storm's still there. You've made your friends uncomfortable and you're apologetic, so what's been accomplished? The storm is there. Accept it. Make the best of it. What else can you do? Laugh. Make a joke of the whole thing (even if you don't think it's that funny). You'll "flow" with it. You'll shrug your shoulders knowing that life has had worse moments. What the heck - the house is still standing and you're not all out in some field. So it really could be worse. You're flowing. You're accepting that which you cannot change. You're learning to go "beyond" what nature or anyone else has tossed into your lap.

"Spiritual." H-m-m, this may not be that simple. Mankind has been trying to define "spirituality" for eons, but here goes: Spirituality is the ability to flow with the universal forces, without those forces being limited by the human ego. The inability to diminish the altered ego very often defeats your purpose.

You are not just a mass of bones and flesh, deposited on this earth and left to sink or swim. You have a direct connection to the force that created this universe. Spirituality is also then, an awareness of the connection and a desire to reach out to it. It's living your life with the knowledge that you have this great force working with you. Because of this knowledge, you can "flow" more, you can "allow", you can accept all that life offers and, if the offering isn't so great, you accept that too, knowing that there are lessons to be learned.

When you accept all life, the quality of your life will improve. There will be fewer and fewer lessons to learn. You'll accept the situations you cannot change. You'll flow and that brings a greater joy into your life. And that's what you're here for.

How do you know you have this connection? The best illustration would be your best friend, your intuition. It has never led you astray. It bombards you constantly, but you're usually too busy to listen or else you don't quite trust your "gut feeling".' Yet it's always there, waiting to help you.

This book is going to help you develop it.

And you thought you were all alone!

"Energies going outward" is merely a matter of flowing. Rather like being carried downstream with the current of the river.

"Energies going inward", that's your reaction to the thunderstorm. You felt much more anger and frustration inwardly than you were expressing outwardly. A fury, unexpressed, creates a thunder- storm within us. Rather like trying to swim upstream against a raging torrent. When your energies go outward, you won't feel anger because you're learning to flow.

We also speak of "man limiting man"; of mankind complicating issues. We take the simplest joys of life and make them complex. Is it done for self-esteem? Conversations consist too often of, "You must; you have to; you should".

These are the very limitations of which we speak. In the realm of gemstones, you may be told you can only wear a stone a certain way, or it must (has to!) be worn in a specific area. Not so. You do whatever feels comfortable for you. Whatever _you_ believe the stone will do, it will. That's a truth.

Here's an example. One day I felt I should wear my onyx (it was a beige and white stone). I knew the onyx protects against negativity, and I felt very protected that night when I was bombarded with someone's frustration and anger. What I didn't know was that it is the

<u>black</u> onyx that protects, not the one I was wearing. Because I believed my stone was helping me, it did.

C H A P T E R   II

GENERAL INFORMATION

ON

GEMSTONES

SHAPE OF STONES AND FLAWS

The shape of the stones doesn't matter, nor do the flaws. Sometimes you can buy a beautiful jewel quality rather inexpensively because it is "flawed".

WHERE THE STONES COME FROM

Stones, to be effective, do not have to come from only one location, although there are different mineral contents in various areas of the earth. To say a stone must come from only one place is like saying you have to live in New York City or Los Angeles because nowhere else counts. That's just man limiting man. As always, your intent is the most important factor.

SYNTHETICS

Synthetics just do not have the same vibrations as the natural stones. That's not to say you shouldn't wear and enjoy them, but the attributes are not the same.

RINGS

Our left hand brings in the universal energies, passes them through us (like a circuit) and goes out the right hand. So a ring worn on the left hand brings in; on the right, it sends out.

FINGERS

It doesn't matter one iota what
finger a stone is worn on. Can you
imagine that the force that created
this universe would ordain that the
index finger must have this stone,
the middle finger is for that one,
and the little finger is for this?
When things become too involved or
complicated, you know that mankind
has decided to make it so.

NECKLACES

Necklaces work best because the
main energy centers of the body
(the chakras) are located from the
base of the torso upward, and the
gemstones are more in contact with
them.

EARRINGS

The only earrings that may cause a problem are natural lapis or sapphires, because of their strong vibration. If you're just starting your acquaintance with the stones, they may take some time to adjust to.

POCKETS AND HANDBAGS

Carrying a stone in your pocket or purse, will help to create an overall balance.

WEARING MORE THAN ONE GEMSTONE

Each stone has its own vibration and they're almost like radar – each will help the area that needs stabilization. Most stones are very compatible, but if you become uncomfortable, wear them on different chains.

CHOOSING A STONE

We're not sure if you choose the stone or it chooses you. You look at a large selection of stones and jewelry and find that you are drawn to one particular stone. Pick it up. If it _feels_ good, buy it. That's the best way to buy gemstones. Go with your intuition. Trust your instincts. Know that you have selected the stone that can help you the most.

As time goes on, you'll add to your "collection". Each day, try to get a "feel" for the stone that will suit you. Or maybe you had a thought that a certain stone should be worn. Do it. The stone you've selected has the qualities needed for that day.

You're developing your intuition and that's one of the best gifts you can give yourself.

LOSING A STONE

When you become attuned to the stones and their attributes, interesting things will happen. One day a stone you've been wearing will make you uncomfortable. Or you'll get the feeling that you should replace it with something else. Do so, or it will fall off its chain, or become lost in some other way. It will seldom break or be lost permanently. You'll know when to begin wearing it again. It's your intuition working to help you. <u>Listen to it</u>. The more you pay heed to it, the stronger it will become.

C H A P T E R   III

CLEANSING

AND

ENERGIZING

GEMSTONES

CLEANSING GEMSTONES

Everything you touch picks up and retains your vibration. People who are very sensitive to vibrations can actually do a "reading" by handling the object. It's known as Psychometry. Let's say you wear a ring so it carries your vibration. But the persons who made it, who sold it, and who gave it to you as a gift, have also left their imprint on the ring. Perhaps it's an antique piece of jewelry or a stone you found. For whatever reason, you want to cleanse the item to remove the energies that are on them.

First, bear in mind, that mankind loves to complicate things. We have interesting attitudes. If it's not expensive, it's not worth much. If it's not hard or complicated, there's something wrong. So how do you cleanse a stone? The same way

you clean yourself and you don't
even need the soap! If a shower or
bath feels great to you, imagine
how the stones and crystals will
love it. No sea salt. No over night
or week long soaks. Do you think
that the force that created this
simple, beautiful universe, that
gave us gems and crystals, would
then deem it necessary for us to go
through rituals in order to cleanse
them? Just use water - which is the
cleanser of the earth, the purifier.
It doesn't even matter if it's tap,
bottled, soft, hard or has chlorine
in it. Whatever your water source,
you feel exhilarated after a shower
- why shouldn't the stones?

ENERGIZING GEMSTONES

Many, many years ago, people faced
the East and worshipped the sun. It
was an acknowledgement of the life
force. In their hands they held
their gemstones so that the sun's
rays could revitalize them. When
they were worn, the gemstones kept
generating their own energy to
blend with the wearer's in order
to balance the body. They blend and
expand your own vibration and
energy as well. Replenish the
stones you have in the same manner.
With few exceptions, which we will
discuss later, put your amethysts,
crystals, sodalites - all your
stones in the sunlight. Just leave
them on the kitchen counter or a
sofa, anywhere where the sun's rays
can revitalize them. Length of
time? Half an hour; a couple of
hours; all day. There's no specific
time. Even on a somewhat cloudy

day, they'll be revitalized.

SPECIAL NOTE: If you have a piece of jewelry that was given to you by someone with whom you are no longer compatible, and seeing or wearing it brings back unhappy memories, either give that piece away or sell it. You can cleanse the stone of that person's vibration, but the memories remain. The stone then represents the past.

C H A P T E R   IV

ASTROLOGICAL

SIGNS

ASTROLOGICAL SIGNS

There is no true birthstone.

If you're a Capricorn, that is not the total person. You have many other aspects. The Capricorn could have a lot of Pisces, Leo, or Virgo in their natal chart.

The two major signs are EARTH and AIR. Most stones, worn as jewelry, fall into these categories.

The other signs, FIRE and WATER also apply their energies.

The FIRE signs have a lot of power, but often have the tendency to over-power. In order to balance within, FIRE signs need the water to gain the capability of under-standing others, rather than the over-powering need to lead others.

EARTH signs, though beautiful, can be a heavier sign within the body. Changeable, temperamental, stubborn. Therefore, the AIR sign helps the EARTH sign to flow to its greatest capacity.

AIR signs have great capabilities, but like the wind, do need the abilities to relate to the earth. The AIR sign has a tendency to flow over the tree tops, always looking beyond. They need the ability to touch earth and stabilize their capabilities.

<u>WATER</u> signs flow easily, but have difficulty with inner strength and inner convictions. The FIRE sign gives the WATER sign more determination.

FIRE signs:

    ARIES, LEO or SAGITTARIUS -

    Bring in the WATER sign -
    pearl, opal, coral.

EARTH signs:

    TAURUS, VIRGO or CAPRICORN -

    Bring in the AIR sign -
    crystal, aquamarine.

AIR signs:

    GEMINI, LIBRA or AQUARIUS -

    Bring in the EARTH sign -
    malachite, jasper, lapis or
    turquoise.

WATER signs:

    CANCER, SCORPIO or PISCES -

    Bring in the FIRE sign -
    carnelian, ruby.

C H A P T E R   V

METALS

METALS

The metals you wear affect your well being, just as colors and gemstones do.

This chapter describes the benefits of gold, silver and other metals because your awareness of their effects is important.

BRASS

Commonly used in jewelry, brass is not conducive for man's growth.

It's very much like lead. It doesn't conduct anything, but it can make the body more dense.

BRONZE

Similar to brass; it's a poor conductor.

COPPER

Copper balances the mineral content of the body.

If someone has arthritis, wearing a copper bracelet will help with the copper deficiency within that person. It will also help the pain to subside.

If you have a cut, put copper on the bandage and it will help relieve the pain.

GOLD

Gold is a <u>tremendous</u> conductor. It <u>magnifies</u> what you're feeling.

When you're feeling vibrant and alive, wear a gold necklace because it will magnify your vibration.

However, if you're tired, not feeling well, angry or frustrated, the gold will pick up every bit of that energy and magnify it.

When you're feeling good, gold will bring a greater serenity.

When you're feeling frustrated, it will bring a greater frustration.

Earrings, bracelets and rings will not effect you as strongly as a necklace (because of the energy centers).

PEWTER

The base is lead, so it's not a conductor as the silver is.

Enjoy it for the loveliness it is.

SILVER

Silver is a stabilizer.

If you're having a day with a great deal of anger or frustration, wear silver and you'll feel calmer and more serene within yourself.

Silver will tap a greater purity.

Silver works very much like the colors blue and grey for calmness and serenity.

If you're feeling rather "down", put silver on, and it will help you stabilize.

WHITE GOLD

It works almost like silver and is a great stabilizer.

You don't have to be as cautious with white gold as you do with the yellow gold.

GOLD, SILVER - AND YOUR TEETH

If you feel you have more "bad" than "good" days, please don't throw out your gold jewelry. Simply develop an awareness of your inner feelings.

It's not a cause for great concern; your body contains elements of gold and silver within it. It's just always <u>there</u>.

If you're like the vast majority, you have silver fillings in your teeth, and perhaps a gold crown or two.

If you're feeling negative, the gold in your mouth will bring in more negativity (bet you're thrilled to hear that), <u>but</u> you probably have more silver, and that will help to stabilize.

CHAPTER VI

COLORS

COLOR

If you think you're not affected by color or gemstones, give this some thought. We "talk" in color: "Boy, was I blue today"; "Wow! Is he ever in a black mood"; "I was seeing red"; "What a sunny disposition"; etc.

You walk into a room and love it. The same room, decorated in different shades, makes you uncomfortable. Did you know that a room painted pink will subdue a violent person?

You live your life reacting to color. It lifts your spirits, gives you more vitality, calms you. What we're learning is that we are definitely affected by color. When we gain the knowledge of what individual colors can do, working with them will certainly enhance our lives.

And gemstones have COLOR.

When you become aware of the balance that is needed by your body, you will become less frustrated and more serene. You're not only helping yourself, family and friends, you're helping the whole universe by sending out a more peaceful vibration.

When you feel good about yourself, you have more love and energy to give to others. When you balance, you help to create the balance within others. It's infectious. You'll become a giver of joy.

Develop an awareness of what color and gemstones someone else may need and perhaps someday you can give them an article of clothing or a stone. The colors and stones work whether anyone is conscious of their attributes or not.

BLACK

Black is beautiful!

When you think of black, it's generally in the negative aspects - death, black magic, depression. The wicked witches from the old fairy tales were always in black. Black became known as heavy, sad, depressing.

Not anymore!

Many, many years ago, when people died, they wrapped the body in a black shroud. Death and black have always been associated together, but they used the black shroud to protect the body from what is called "the lower astral entities", little mischievous goblins and ghosts, so that the body would not be disturbed.

They knew, long ago, that black protects us. It creates a shield around us, a buffer zone.

The best time to put on something black is after you've meditated, because it will encase what you're feeling. If you're tired, grouchy or not feeling well, it will encase that too.

If there's a lot of negativity in your home, or office, or wherever, wear a black stone.

If you know someone who is too open and absorbs all the energies of others, give them a black stone so that they won't be bombarded.

Tarot cards and crystal balls are often wrapped in black to protect their energy fields.

There is no conflict between the black and other stones. It's a

protective source that the other
stones work well with.

Think of black as the sentinel —
the shield — the protector.

BLUE

Blue has to do with knowledge, sharing, calming, cooling, flowing and anything to do with speech, such as vocal expression, communication.

Blue is the color of the fifth energy center (chakra) - the throat.

If you are feeling a little upset, a bit nervous, apprehensive or frustrated, wear blue for it will help calm you. Don't wear red at this time.

Blue will also help you to say what you're feeling; freely, without frustration, anger or helplessness. This means your energies are flowing outward.

Blue helps in another way too. When someone feels that they're always right - and you have to do things _their_ way - it means they're not flowing. Give them something blue.

When you know someone having any of these problems, suggest that they wear blue (or give them a sodalite) and tell them how good they look in that color. Suggest they wear it more often. You are helping them to balance.

BROWN

Brown is an earth color.

It helps one attune to the environment and the earth.

Brown gives an appreciation of the flowers, trees, shrubs, etc.

If you're in a "brown-beige" stage of your life, one day you'll start to notice sunrises, or be especially appreciative of flowers. You may find yourself buying more houseplants. You'll develop more of an <u>awareness</u> of nature.

It's a joy that will never leave you.

GREEN

Green has to do with the emotions —
the heart.

Green is a giver. It flows outward.

Green is the color of the fourth
energy center — the heart.

Green has a soothing, healing
effect, and it will balance you.

You will work with less emotion, and
more compassion.

Wear green when:

> People keep dumping their
> problems on you and you give
> away too much of your energy
> in sympathy and drain yourself.

> You're frustrated by other
> peoples' emotions.

> You need to go beyond the
> emotional level of another
> person.

In each of these situations, you're working with too much of <u>your</u> emotions.

GREY

Grey is a stabilizer.

Grey is the balancer of the positive and negative forces within you.

If you're frustrated or angry, reach for grey or silver.

Grey is serenity.

LILAC

Lilac is a balancer.

It is the wisdom of temperance.

Lilac creates the inner wisdom of tolerance that one does not verbally destroy another to redeem one's pride.

PALE LAVENDER

If the lavender and the lilac are very light shades, they have a pink base and would affect you as pink does.

ORANGE

Orange is life. Zest.

Orange has an energy that produces a useful approach to life - less worry.

Orange is the color of the second energy center - the sensual; the sacral center.

Orange is the fire of life with the aid of stability.

Orange is sexy.

PINK

Pink is universal love.

Pink is loving and being loved.

Pink enables you to love yourself, thus enabling you to love another. So pink is for self-love.

Pink draws more love to you and you feel more loving (although you're not always totally aware of it).

When you're wearing pink, you feel calmer, protected, more loving and serene.

Any stone that has pink in it has love and radiates it.

PURPLE

Purple is the light of understanding and tolerance.

A wonderful balancer of the energy centers within the body.

Purple represents the spiritual awakening.

It helps to keep tempers in check.

Purple also gives you an extra strength to go beyond cravings.

Purple is the color of the seventh energy center - the crown.

RED

When you need energy - wear red.

If you're angry or frustrated, do not wear red. It will enhance it.

Don't wear red when you have too much energy.

Red is the color of the first energy center at the base of the spine; the root chakra.

You'll notice that people who are angry, quite often wear red. They're attuned to that "fire".

If you need to be "perked up", wear red. It will brighten your day.

TURQUOISE

Turquoise helps the mind and body flow more easily with life.

Turquoise is the blue of the sky, the green of the earth (plants) and a bit of black for protection.

Turquoise will help you extend your energies (vibrations). A beautiful attunement.

WHITE

White is purity, innocence.

White is the color (non-color) that fills the body with a new vibratory transformation.

White can heal cells. White is mental transformation. White <u>is</u> total transformation.

White is reflected light containing all of the visible rays of the spectrum.

Wearing white helps to produce a <u>lighter</u> outlook.

In meditation, reach for the white light. Surround yourself in it. <u>Feel</u> it enter through the seventh energy center, the crown.

C H A P T E R   VII

GEMSTONES

AGATE

The agate is an earth stone.

It would help to balance someone
who uses logic much more than
intuition.

It will help to stabilize and bring
the two areas together more easily.

When you do not want to become
involved in limitations, "This is
logically right or this is logically
wrong", wear an agate.

AGATE: EARTH sign.

GREY AGATE

Serenity.
Earth Balance
Love.
Spirituality.

Grey allows the white (universal)
force to flow through more easily.

GREY AGATE: EARTH sign.

AMAZONITE

An aqua colored stone, mostly available in beads for necklaces.

An amazonite is a balancer of the emotions.

It works somewhat like the rose quartz, but it flows more with the emotions towards others (rather than the self-love).

AMAZONITE: EARTH sign.

AMBER

Amber is the blood source; the resin of trees.

It heals the blood of man.

It helps the blood by purifying the basic human emotions of the first and second energy centers; thereby reducing high blood pressure.

AMBER: EARTH sign.

AMETHYST

An amethyst is most powerful when worn at the throat area.

An amethyst helps rid you of cravings - drugs, smoking, sweets, alcohol, etc.

It will stabilize all the energy centers of the body.

It will help you get rid of fears.

An amethyst helps to open the third "eye" because it raises the spiritual level.

If someone's ego is a bit too big, give them an amethyst to wear, because it creates a spiritual response.

An amethyst is a quartz crystal.

The dense amethyst would be very
good for someone who wants to
become more spiritual, but has not
totally balanced their earth
vibration.

AMETHYST: AIR sign - If it's clear
            (can see through)

            EARTH sign - if it's
            dense.

AQUAMARINE

It's a water stone and like water,
has a lot of magnetism.

It flows like water and when you
wear it, you flow more and the
stabilization becomes greater.

It flows, allowing a FIRE or EARTH
sign to take time to see the
abilities of others.

It has a wondrous affect on you.

An aquamarine need not be a single,
expensive stone. There are aquamarine chip necklaces available at
a reasonable price.

AQUAMARINE: AIR sign.

AVENTURINE

Aventurine is a soft, light green color.

This stone has a gentle, stabilizing effect that works on the heart (emotional) area.

An excellent gift for a young person.

Although it works on a different energy center, it is similar to the moonstone for the stabilization it will create.

AVENTURINE: EARTH sign.

AZURITE - MALACHITE

This combination of azurite and malachite creates a very, very powerful stone.

It has an unique and distinctive coloration of principally blues and greens, with flecks of aqua, black and other hues as well.

Azurite-Malachite helps cells within to transform. Your unique talents are intensified for the good of self and others.

Use it when you want to be a channel for healing; when you want to heal yourself physically; when you want to heal emotions.

A rare stone in that it will help to heal cancer if the person has developed a spiritual awareness.

This stone will also intensify the vibration for healing, like a surging forward.

Azurite-malachite is now available in heart shapes, drops and necklaces.

An azurite, placed under a pillow, will intensify your dreams and your recall of them.

AZURITE-MALACHITE: EARTH sign.

BLOODSTONE

The bloodstone is basically a green stone (jasper) flecked with red.

It can give a greater strength and self-confidence.

The bloodstone is a powerful healing stone that must be used sparingly. The healing must begin with the spiritual vibration of the healer, his intent. It then can be used on the patient to balance the matter of the body and the anti-matter of the etheric.

You can apply it directly to the body. Use the stone in a clock-wise circular motion three times; then counter clock-wise three times to attune the body to the etheric. That's all. Once a day would be enough.

But if the person channeling the healing is worried, frustrated or feeling pain, those emotions would limit the capabilities of the stone. The healer must have compassion and clear intent, not the process of proving their capabilities as a healer (someone coming from "ego"), or the stone will unbalance the healer's vibration.

BLOODSTONE: EARTH sign.

BLUE LACE AGATE

This stone works on the thyroid so it's most powerful when worn at the throat area.

The blue lace agate brings a total attunement to the senses.

You're going to hear more, feel more and your touch is going to become more sensitive.

BLUE LACE AGATE: AIR sign (clearer)

EARTH sign (dense)

BLUE TOPAZ

You know those wonderful ideas you sometimes get - they're not a "feeling" like your intuitive - but a "thought" or "idea" that suddenly enters your mind (another example of your connection to the force that created this universe). Well, the blue topaz helps you to become more of a receiver.

Blue topaz has to do with sound - the sounds of the universe.

It picks up thought forms from the clearer vibration of other dimensions. One then works with the power of constructive vibration and the blue topaz helps you attune to those constructive patterns of the universe.

This is another stone that need not be too expensive. The less costly ones are paler in color, but work just as well.

BLUE TOPAZ: AIR sign.

CARNELIAN

This stone has a great vibrancy and will give you the courage and stability to go forward.

The carnelian works best when worn over the heart area. The rays then begin to open up the throat area as well. It creates an emotional balance which helps one express their feelings better.

Do you know someone who is very vibrant, very beautiful, very giving, yet rather insecure about themselves? With all the love they give to others, everything seems to go wrong for them. They give - but they don't know how to give to self. A carnelian will produce a new strength within them. The fire of this stone will help to stabilize and lift their vibration.

When someone has a lot of depth, a lot of knowledge, but they're afraid to step forward, the carnelian lights a fire under them.

If someone is a giver, but they get into a deep slump when things don't go together, the carnelian will uplift and stabilize them.

A wonderful stone for an energy boost.

CARNELIAN: EARTH sign, but it functions a bit as a FIRE sign.

CHRYSOCOLLA

This is a green-aqua stone with dark flecks.

The chrysocolla is a beautiful vibration that can help balance thought and body.

CHRYSOCOLLA: EARTH sign.

CHRYSOPRASE

The coloration of the chrysoprase is a soft, but distinctive green.

This stone is available in drops and heart shapes for pendants.

The chrysoprase works with the emotional balance of the heart area, in a manner similar to the jade.

It also works in the area of the solar plexus allowing the intuitive to balance and become stronger.

CHRYSOPRASE: EARTH sign.

CINNABAR

Cinnabar is a red carved stone that looks not only Oriental in design, but looks as if it was made of wood.

It's created from a mercury and sulfide process and can be extremely toxic if worn next to the skin - so avoid bracelets and earrings without a backing.

The mercury within the stone will allow a person to flow.

If someone is just starting the process of growth, do not give them this stone, because if they become angry, it could enhance the anger (the red and the mercury).

CINNABAR: EARTH sign.

CITRINE

This stone is a member of the crystal family.

The <u>soft yellow/orange citrine</u> gives added energy and emotional balance.

The <u>green dyed citrine</u> works on the gall bladder and liver areas (similar to the peridot).

CITRINE: AIR sign.

CORAL

Coral is a wonderful stabilizer and all the corals carry the negative ion. For further information on the benefits of the negative ions, see "Pearls".

BLACK CORAL

The protector. Wards off negativity. Creates a shield around you.

PINK CORAL

Although a salmon shade, it has a pink, not a red, base.

This stone, flecked with white, has the vibrancy that improves one's self-image most quickly, adding to your self worth. Remember, pink is love.

RED CORAL

It will enhance a person's energy (red).

WHITE CORAL

Self-image, purity and all the attributes of the white color.

CORALS: WATER sign.

CRYSTALS

The crystal, quartz crystal, and the double-terminated crystals are <u>all</u> quartz crystals, and have the same <u>basic</u> qualities. There is a difference with the minerals in the earth as there is with all stones.

The crystal is a "giver" and will enhance anything you're feeling, so be careful. If you're depressed, unhappy, or nervous, it will enhance that too. It's not fussy.

It works with the electrical energies and, if you're a <u>very</u> negative person, it could give you a burn.

It's a great power builder and brings in the power of the universe. The person who wears it begins to purify.

94

The crystal opens up the sixth energy center, the "third eye", as does the amethyst.

The crystal will not take on your vibration. It will enhance it.

It is not a good gift for a young person because they fluctuate so much in their emotions, and the crystal will enhance that.

CRYSTALS FOR HEALING

There are many quartz crystals: the amethyst, citrine, smokey quartz, etc. The amethyst has an iron content, the rose quartz has a minute bit of titanium; but what we're discussing here is the clear quartz crystal.

Most stones have a tremendous electro-magnetic field; the crystal does not. The power is contained within the crystal. This is what makes it totally unique and, if you struck and crushed the crystal, you would have a tremendous amount of voltage.

The vibration of the holder of the crystal being used for healing is vitally important. If a person is doing the healing to elevate their ego, it can back-fire. If someone is feeling, "I am the healer; I have the crystal; I will do this; I will do that; look at me; I'm going to do it", it will create greater problems for this person. What happens is that the vortex of the person gets into the vortex of the crystal. The crystal becomes more powerful, but it works in a negative way because the thought processes were negative. Remember, the crystal is a magnifier, and so finely attuned to one's thought processes, one must be very sure that the healer's ego is not elevated to the point that they limit the crystal's work.

Almost all quartz crystals have one terminated end. This simply means that one end has its beginning in the earth minerals. Therefore, the flow stems from the earth base to the terminated end. The terminated end is pointed and can have four or more plane faces. Although it may look as if it were faceted by a jeweler, it is a totally natural formation; it was created this way.

If you decide to use the crystal, or any other stone or method for healing, always know that you are not the healer, simply a channel or instrument for healing. The universal forces do the healing, and by your loving intent, you want to be used by those forces for this purpose. When you see several successful healings, be careful that you don't fall into the trap of "I did this healing; I healed so-and-so; I, I, I." (Our alter-ego has a wonderful "me first" attitude so sometimes you just have to swat it on the head.) There are many people who are famous as healers, and they are healers, because they have never lost sight of the fact that they are channels for healing and this is what makes them so continually effective. Each day say to yourself, "I want to be used as a channel for healing" and you'll be amazed at the wonderful results.

There's an exercise you might do before you channel a healing; it's a quick method of "centering" yourself. Inhale deeply, hold for the count of three and exhale slowly. Do this three times. That's it! You'll feel so relaxed and serene! Do this any time you feel tense or frustrated. Several times a day if you need to. It's one of the good things you can do for yourself.

After you have "centered", hold the crystal in your left hand (this is the hand that brings in the universal energies), terminated end pointing outward, and if there is love and caring within you, the healing takes place. You simply ask to be used as an instrument for healing; you ask that the bodily function (whatever it is that needs the healing) be returned to normal; that it go from a negative to a positive. Remember to always say "thank you", because you <u>are</u> thankful that you've been used as a channel. There are times when it will appear that the healing has not taken place. Remember that the combined forces of the universe, flowing through the healer and crystal, cut off the process that feeds the illness, thus allowing it to heal in its own time, rather than instantaneously. <u>A</u> healing has taken place; never doubt it. It may be that the person with the illness can now handle the pain more easily. <u>Do not</u> take it as a personal failure. You weren't doing the healing; you were a channel.

The crystal is an instrument that can transform any body. The crystal is absorbing the universal forces and sending it out the terminated end. You can even place the terminated end on the area that needs the healing. <u>Feel</u> the energies from the crystal going outward and entering the area.

THE DOUBLE TERMINATED CRYSTAL

THE HERKIMER DIAMOND

The double terminated crystal, which grows in many parts of the earth, is most commonly known on the East Coast, as the Herkimer Diamond, and is mined in the general area of Herkimer, New York.

The Herkimer is easily distinguished from regular quartz crystals because it is water-clear, with a clarity and brightness not usually found in other crystals. It is a most brilliant crystal, with short prism faces and the highest refractive index.

The regular quartz crystal is grounded with the minerals of the earth; it grows from that. The double terminated crystal grows in an entirely different manner. It is in a vaporized, gaseous level, not attached to the ground on any level until it grows tremendously. It's doubly terminated because it grows in a "womb". It is not grounded, or from the ground, as most crystals are.

If one is spiritually motivated (letting go of ego), the Herkimer or double terminated crystal begins to balance the body and the etheric (energy or electro-magnetic field) with a greater force.

When one is ego motivated, the crystal will enhance the body until the body burns itself out with a vibration of over-production. In other words, the cells will begin to function in such a fast manner that the cells will destroy self. One needs the balance of matter and anti-matter to function to the fullest capabilities.

The Herkimer Diamond is unique in that it can reverse polarity. It has the ability to change positive to negative within itself. It also creates this in terms of healing. If there is a cut to be healed, it is in the negative vibration. The crystal's need is to change its force to a positive, in order to heal and balance the cut. The double terminated crystal has a greater power to bring in the light, or universal force, to heal from either end and create the positive-negative balance within the person.

AUSTRIAN CRYSTALS

These crystals are beautifully faceted and often seen hanging in windows as well as used for pendants and earrings.

A high degree of lead oxide has been combined in the glass to soften it, thus enabling it to be cut and faceted precisely.

It has a unique vibration and, although different, can be used somewhat like the quartz crystal. It doesn't have quite the same power, but it is a clarity of power.

Some of these crystals are faceted with an end quite pointed and used as pendulums.

Hang an Austrian crystal in a sunny window and enjoy the rainbows it will create.

DIAMONDS

The diamond takes on, and holds, the vibrations around it.

The diamond is a very powerful stone, but if there's frustration or negativity, and you're wearing it at the throat area, it can create too much energy; too much power.

Energy enters through the left hand and goes out the right, like a circuit. If you're frustrated, and the diamond pendant has picked it up, it's blocking the energy flow.

There's no problem wearing diamonds on your fingers or in earrings.

If you feel the diamond is holding negativity, just cleanse it.

Because the diamond holds the

vibrations around it, just imagine how wonderful that is when you're feeling really terrific!

DIAMOND: AIR sign.

THE HOPE DIAMOND

A diamond holds negativity.

The Hope Diamond was stolen many,
many times, and there's been much
death and violence associated with
it. That beautiful stone is holding
that negativity.

Since 1958, when the Hope Diamond
came to the United States, you'll
notice that the negativity has
expanded in this country.

It is said to be the only stone
that, when X-rayed, turns a brilliant red because of the anger and
negativity contained in it.

The only way the Hope Diamond could
be changed would be to submerge it
in water, and let the water cleanse
the vibration.

What you can do personally for the Hope Diamond, would be to surround it in pink light, which is love. And it has been said that love can change all things!

DOLOMITE

This peach colored stone works on the stomach area.

The dolomite brings inner peace and less confusing constrictions to the stomach - in other words, it's great for someone with ulcers or any nervous stomach condition.

The dolomite is not a jewelry item, but a stone to be held during meditation.

Available in rock shops.

EMERALD

The emerald is definitely a healing
stone.

The vibration of the emerald goes
right into the inner organs.

It heals spiritually, physically
and chemically.

If someone is attuned to the
universe, but they are busy deciding
what they don't like, too busy to
decide what they do like, an
emerald would be very good for them.

As with most stones, place it in
the sun every day or two, so it can
be replenished by the sun's rays.

An emerald can help to stabilize a
back problem - one that is caused
when people are emotionally upset
and buying into other peoples'

emotions and they haven't the strength to step forward. It's almost like the back takes on a difficulty that makes it almost impossible to step forward.

If you want to use an emerald for a physical healing (let's say you have a cut on your leg), place the emerald so that the sunlight passes through it and direct that light toward the cut.

EMERALD: AIR or EARTH sign, depend-
          ing on the density.

EPIDOTE

The epidote contains a lot of green flecked with orange.

Promotes self-love.

It helps to balance one's self toward a healing vibration.

The epidote is not a healing stone for others, but a stone used by the healer for self. When one is on the spiritual, caring path, the epidote helps the healer to center his energies more quickly so that the higher forces come through.

EPIDOTE: EARTH sign.

FLUORITE

The fluorite is a stone without the clarity of an amethyst or aquamarine, yet because of its distinct terminals, it is a good conductor of energies.

It's a wonderful stone for meditation, because it will energize the body.

Now available in jewelry.
Also available at rock shops.

FLUORITE: AIR sign.

GARNET

The garnet works with the energy center at the base of the spine (root) and the nerves along the spinal column. This is the area known as your security level.

The garnet can be worn by anyone who is insecure; and that insecurity can stem from the time you were two, five or ten years old. You may not even have a conscious awareness of the cause of it. However, if that energy center is "threatened" in any way, you may find yourself with a backache and you can't figure out why you have it.

The garnet is also an excellent stone for someone who appears judgmental. "I don't like this." "Do it this way."

The garnet can definitely be used to relieve pain.

If you have a lot of back or neck aches, wearing a garnet necklace for a few weeks will dispel the pain.

Remember, you take in with the left (negative) and give out with the right (positive).

Anytime you have pain, if you put your right hand on the area, you will intensify it, because the right is a "THRUST". Always use the left hand, because it will transform the energy.

To relieve spine or neck pain, center yourself, using the breathing exercise explained under "Crystals". Get into a meditative state. Take the LEFT hand and place it on the area of the pain. Take the RIGHT hand, with the garnet in it, and put it on the lower back. You're

creating a positive exchange, a
total circuit, with your hands and
the garnet. Do this for about ten
minutes, twice a day, and you'll
find the garnet's great rays are
actually transmitted into the area
of the spinal column.

When you use both hands in this
manner, you're also reaching out to
the emotional cause of the condition
and effecting a change on that
level as well.

Using one hand alone does not
create a circuit, but it will
relieve the pain. Center yourself,
relax into a meditative state, put
the garnet in your LEFT hand and
place it on the area that hurts.
Begin to feel the whole you expand-
ing and know that the long rays of
the garnet are healing your own
body, stabilizing it. Do this for
five or ten minutes, twice a day,
and within three weeks you'll

wonder where the back pain went. Not because you've healed it, but by using the garnet and meditating, you've disbursed the energy that collected at the base of the spine - your security level.

You can also lie down and put the garnet on the lower back (use the left hand) and no matter how small the garnet, the power of the ray will help to balance the area.

When you're doing the healings, visualize the white light entering your body through the top of your head, coming down the spinal column, and rolling around the base of the spine.

If you choose, you can also rub the garnet a little bit, up and down on the spine.

These garnets for healing need not be faceted stones. Most rock shops will have garnets in rough form, usually circular, inexpensive, and an excellent size to be held for healings.

The denser garnet will help to balance the earthly vibration of a person.

The lighter garnet, if someone is reaching for more spiritual awareness, will help their security level.

GARNET: AIR sign (if light and clear).

EARTH sign (if dense).

GREEN GARNET

Works like the peridot, but more difficult to locate and very expensive.

GREEN GARNET: EARTH sign (dense).

AIR sign (light).

GOLDSTONE

This is not a natural stone, but it does have the vibration needed for spiritual growth because of the coloration.

The goldstone works in a manner similar to carnelian, but it does transmit more sound to the body. Because of the gold, it's a transmitter, so it does have a high vibration.

If someone is just beginning to know the value of who they are, the carnelian would be better for them than the goldstone. But, if they've had this awareness for some time, and they're feeling a little "down", the goldstone would help them. (Similar to the "fire" of the carnelian.)

The goldstone is a deep, but soft, orange tone, heavily flecked with gold.

GOLDSTONE: The color of it is the EARTH, but with higher vibrational lights. Similar to the dense amethyst, it can begin to process stabilization within a person.

BLUE GOLDSTONE

The blue goldstone is not a natural stone.

It has an unique coloration of being blue/black and heavily flecked with silver.

Like the goldstone, it sparkles with life and lights.

The blue goldstone brings in the need for greater wisdom and understanding of self.

It helps you "unblock" the fifth energy center, the throat, which is expression.

BLUE GOLDSTONE: EARTH sign.

HALITE

Halite is rock salt, dyed pink. Some of the larger pieces have rose and plum shades as well.

The specimen is attractive and readily available in rock shops.

Halite is not meant to be worn. Simply placed in a room, it will radiate a gentle love vibration, eventually changing the vibration of the room.

An excellent gift for a young person who needs that stable vibration. A good gift for anyone who needs more love in their lives.

A word of caution - do not wash Halite under hot water! After all, it's salt!

HEMATITE

Hematite is a very dark grey with a
silvery cast.

It has more "heft", or weight, to
it than most stones.

Hematite works on the neurons of
the brain and the solar plexus; the
intuition.

Wearing it brings a greater attunement. It has a great deal of
magnetism and will draw in the
energy of the universe.

Hold it in your left hand for
meditation.

It's an excellent stone for people
who are very logical, who have to
have everything explained to them,
because as they wear it, it will
strengthen their intuition, the gut

reaction.

Available in necklaces, earrings and inexpensive drops.

HEMATITE: EARTH sign (if dense).

AIR sign (if lighter).

IVORY FOR JEWELRY

When the Indians, and other tribes, hunted, they used every part of the animal, for their survival depended on it.

There was a very reverent exchange.

No animal was killed for the sport of it or for it's tusks.

When you have an animal that's killed for the ivory, you have enzymes of fear going all through the bones.

Today, there are controls to prevent the needless slaughter of animals, but we would suggest you hold the ivory piece in your hand. If it feels good, buy it. But if it makes you uncomfortable - well, use your intuition.

JADE

Jade works with the emotional balance of the heart area, same as the chrysoprase or the green onyx.

Jade is a cleansing, healing, comforting vibration.

Wearing jade will give you more patience.

If you're a little upset, a jade will calm you.

A jade takes you to a level of calmness; less re-action. Then the body can heal itself.

If you want to be a channel for healing, but are unsure of yourself, insecure about projecting yourself as a healer, wear a green stone. It will enhance the healing energy.

If you've no one to practice healing on, take in the power of the universe - and heal the universe itself. Channel a healing to your dog. Your cat. A houseplant. It doesn't have to be a specific person. Send healing to anyone creating a great controversy upon the earth.

If you practice everyday, you're building a balance within the receiving and the giving out. When you then channel a healing to a person, you'll feel much more confident and the healing will go very well.

All jades (yellow, Burma, white, lavender, Soo Chow) are stabilizers. All have the ability to calm and stabilize the body.

Jade does not change the internal body. It changes the electro-magnetic field which in turn changes the inner body.

In other words, if you're upset,
that's reflected in your "field".
The jade will change the field,
producing a calmness, and that will
be reflected back to your physical
body.

JADE: EARTH sign.

JASPER

The jasper has a tremendous variety of colors.

The jasper has the earth vibration.

It helps to stabilize the emotions.

It's not as powerful as the rhodochrosite, but it does work a little toward uniting the sub-conscious and the conscious self.

RED JASPER

This is also a stabilizer, but adds a bit more energy (red).

JASPER: EARTH sign.

LABRADORITE

Labradorite is a deep grey, but very opalescent with bright flashes of mainly greens and blues.

This stone will work, in a minute manner, for total balancing. Where some stones work on particular organs, such as the peridot, the labradorite will not. But what it is doing is feeding every cell within the organ, within the space between the organs, within every cell, but in a minute balancing manner - slowly and steadily.

The labradorite will bring a great deal of serenity to the wearer.

Available in labradorite chip necklaces.

LABRADORITE: EARTH sign.

LAPIS LAZULI

Almost azure blue in shading, with flecks of gold (pyrite).

Greatly used in the breastplates of the ancient powerful rulers.

<u>Natural</u> lapis has a very high vibration and is excellent for stabilizing the heart.

It will diminish frustration.

It will stabilize the fifth energy center, the throat (speech).

It will stabilize the fourth energy center, the heart (emotions).

It will stabilize the second center, the sacral (the ego).

The lapis will continue on to stabilize all the other energy centers, so that none overpowers another - in other words, a total balancing.

Wearing a lapis will help you to become a channel.

Lapis can be expensive in necklaces, but it is available in heart shapes and crosses, which are less expensive.

LAPIS: EARTH sign.

LEOPARD SKIN AGATE

The leopard skin beads have an almost mottled look, basically with shades of grey and black. To this are added other shades of pinks, yellows, etc.

We will describe the leopard skin with the pink cast.

It will enhance your total vibration.

It's a wonderful stabilizer for the heart and solar plexus (intuition) areas.

The leopard skin will help to stabilize your frustrations.

It brings serenity (grey), protection (black), and love (pink).

LEOPARD SKIN AGATE: EARTH sign.

MALACHITE

Be wary of the malachite. It can have a negative or positive vibration.

It has the green of healing and the black of protection, but it's not a stone you would wear every day.

If you're feeling very good about yourself, the malachite could be a tremendous healer of your own body, specifically the pancreas and the spleen.

Look at the stone. If it feels good to you, wear it. If for any reason you are hesitant, forget it for that day.

A piece of malachite in the bedroom helps rid you of nightmares.

MALACHITE: EARTH sign.

MALACHITE/CHRYSOCOLLA

Mostly available in rock shops as a specimen.

One side will be polished and the colors are various shadings of greens, blues and black, with flecks of browns.

With this combination, you have the process of keeping out negativity (the black) and the process of growth, healing, and balancing.

Hold it in your left hand for meditations.

When one is <u>ready</u>, it will enhance the cells of the body to accept a higher vibration.

MOONSTONE

To revitalize a moonstone, place it in the moonlight of a moon reaching its fullness, not a full or waning moon.

It works with the second energy center (the sensual) organs.

Many, many years ago it was used to aid child-birthing. The moonstones were placed on the abdomen of the pregnant woman; the baby picked up the vibration transmitted to the cells of the woman and the whole process allowed the passage of the baby to come more easily.

It's an excellent stone for meditation because it helps to relieve frustration.

A moonstone will enhance every aspect of the body.

A woman having cramps or discomfort could wear it, or lie down and place it on her abdomen to relieve the pain.

The moonstone will also stabilize the pain from an ovary or prostate problem.

A moonstone will relieve the frustration of menopause, creating a balance within the body.

Young teen-agers are often on an emotional elevator. "I'll just kill myself if Joe doesn't call." "I can't go to school. My hair looks terrible." One minute everything is wonderful; the next minute every-thing is falling apart. A moonstone is a wondrous gift for a teen-ager because it will create the balance needed.

We would suggest that you not give an opal or a crystal to a young

person. It won't provide the
stabilization they need.

PINK MOONSTONE

Although called a "pink" moonstone,
it's much more a salmon shade.

It works as the coral does to
improve your image of your self-
worth.

BLACK MOONSTONE

Much more grey than black, it gives
a greater ability to flow.

Like silver, serenity.

All the moonstones give a great
stabilization; an easing of frustrations.

MOONSTONE: WATER sign (dense).

    AIR sign (clearer).

OBSIDIANS
AND CELLULAR CHANGES

When you decide to become more spiritual, to accept, to allow, to let go of ego, your vibration will become lighter. As this occurs, your physical body will have to adjust to the new vibration.

You may experience headaches, feelings of exhaustion, blemishes, weight changes, etc. This is not a one-time occurrence. It will happen many times because as you "grow", you develop a deeper awareness of the universal forces. The more you "flow", the lighter your vibration will become.

The obsidians, though they are glass created from volcanic ash, will help you through the transitions. There's a tremendous power of transformation in the "stone".

When you're experiencing a cellular change, carry an obsidian, because it will temper the transition; help your body to accept the higher vibration.

The obsidians have a black base, which as you now know, helps to keep out negativity.

GOLDEN SHEEN OBSIDIAN

It looks exactly as the name implies, black with a beautiful golden sheen.

It will enhance your vibration, help the cellular structure, keep out negativity, and help you to flow. Gold enhances what you're feeling, magnifies it, so while going through the cellular change, be a bit careful with this stone.

SNOWFLAKE OBSIDIAN

Black with white "snowflakes".

As this stone helps you to balance the cellular changes, it calls upon a greater power because of the white snowflake.

OBSIDIANS: EARTH sign.

ONYX

The most common coloration is white, beige, salmon, grey, and green. These are often found shaped into bookends, donkeys, ashtrays, turtles, vases, etc.

The very light onyx has a very unusual quality. Worn, or placed near someone as an ornament, it will start them on a spiritual path - without their being aware of it.

Cameo jewelry is generally carved from onyx.

ONYX: EARTH sign.

BLACK ONYX

Often dyed, this stone, as well as the black serpentine or black jet, will give you total protection.

Black is the shield around you; it's your sentinel.

If there's negativity in your home or office (or elsewhere), these black stones will protect you.

BLACK ONYX: EARTH sign.

BLUE ONYX

This onyx is a dyed stone.

The shade of blue is unusual and unlike any other stone.

The blue onyx works in a similar manner to the sodalite.

The blue onyx helps one to communicate without dumping out frustration on another.

It allows what must be said to be transmitted in a less emotional, more loving manner.

BLUE ONYX: EARTH sign

GREEN ONYX

This is also a dyed stone, but, as with the blue onyx, the color is unusual and very distinctive.

This stone works on the fourth energy center - the heart. It is a healer of the emotions.

The green onyx is not as strong a vibration as the emerald, yet it works in a similar manner.

GREEN ONYX: EARTH sign.

OPAL

The opal is the dance of fire, the dance of liquid.

This may sound a bit confusing, but it's a moonstone that's also a FIRE sign although it has a high content of water.

If you're feeling ill, the opal will reflect it and become almost colorless.

It creates a tremendous building process because it's connected with the moon.

It helps to open the "third eye".

The opal enhances whatever you're feeling. If you're unsure of yourself, or judgmental, that's sporadic energy and the opal will enhance all of it. It will then create a pressure too uncomfortable to bear.

Worn on the left hand, it will bring in the universal energies. If worn around the throat, it will open the fifth energy center.

The opal is not a stone to be given to a young person. The fire of the opal will not help anyone whose energy is in any way sporadic.

The moonstone is very stable. The opal is not, depending on who's wearing it.

It's been called an "unlucky" stone, but perhaps those wearing it did not have stable vibrations, so of course it created or added to their problems.

OPAL: WATER sign.
       But it does have EARTH and
       FIRE, too.

PEARLS, MOTHER-OF-PEARLS, FRESH WATER PEARLS AND SEED OR RICE PEARLS

These pearls are vastly different and come to us from a variety of locations around the world.

But they all have the same vibration.

It doesn't matter if you buy a single pearl worth hundreds of dollars, or a mother-of-pearl necklace for six dollars; if it comes from the ocean or fresh water - they all carry the same benefit - the negative ion.

Too many positive ions can upset someone's emotional balance. The full moon and an abundance of positive ions go hand-in-hand.

Did you ever have those days when you prayed you'd arrive home safely because it seemed that half the cars on the road were aiming at you? Check your calendar. It's probably a full moon and all those positive ions.

Most people feel absolutely wonderful when they're by the water and it can be a lake, ocean or a brook. They don't know why, but they just _feel_ good. The same thing happens if you're in a grove of pine trees. You find yourself inhaling deeply and feeling very peaceful - serene.

So now you know. Water and pine groves are among the many things that have negative ions. And you can _never_ have too many negative ions.

The pearls, carrying the negative ion, help asthma and allergy sufferers to breathe more easily.

The pearls are stabilizers and purifiers of energies. The negative ion is the balancer for the body.

Let's say a child is "hyper", fluctuating back and forth with their emotions. Wearing the pearl will help them balance. When they're calm, the negative ion will expand their vibrations.

The pearl blends with any stone in that it is a purifier of energies. However, if it's worn with a diamond that has deep charges of negativity, that diamond will overpower the pearl's abilities.

PEARLS: WATER sign.

PERIDOT

The peridot is a clear green stone with a great deal of yellow in it.

This stone works primarily on two energy centers, the heart (green) and the solar plexus (yellow).

The peridot is definitely a healing stone. It heals gall bladder and liver conditions.

If someone just can't seem to expand their intuitive level, they could meditate with the peridot in the left hand.

If you have a flu or intestinal virus, get into a meditative state and put the peridot on your abdomen for about ten minutes. It will relieve the pain.

PERIDOT: AIR sign.

RHODOCHROSITE

This stone is basically pink, but not a vibrant pink, with flecks of white and black or brown. It has more of an earthy look to it, similar to the jasper.

The rhodochrosite is an unusual stone in that it unites the conscious and the subconscious. It helps to clear out some of the pains, memories, and hurts that are stored in the sub-conscious. It takes some of the fire away from the conscious self, enabling you to flow more easily.

The rhodochrosite helps to raise the consciousness.

You can purchase rhodochrosite chip necklaces and pendants rather inexpensively.

RHODOCHROSITE: EARTH sign.

RHODOLITE

The rhodolite is a garnet from India.

Because of the mineral content of the soil, it has a little more iron in it and produces an almost "plum" shade which is very attractive.

Its benefits are the same as the garnet.

RHODOLITE: EARTH sign.

RHODONITE

The rhodonite is an unusual pink shade, flecked with black.

This is another very, very powerful stone.

It works in a similar fashion to the coral. It raises the self-worth, but it has the blackness to ward off negativity.

The rhodonite works principally on the first three energy centers; your stability ; your self-worth; your ability to understand your intuitive sense.

RHODONITE: EARTH sign.

ROSE QUARTZ

It's pink - it's love.

It's a gentle awakening.

Rose quartz has a very easy, very beautiful, very gentle vibration.

Rose quartz enables you to move gradually into the realization of love.

A great transition stone and an excellent gift for anyone, especially a young person. You're giving a gift of love. How can you beat that?

ROSE QUARTZ: EARTH sign (dense)

                AIR sign (clear)

ROYAL AZEL

A newly "discovered" stone.

It appears to be just a transformation of a more earthly stone in the
jasper-agate family.

Just as mankind is constantly
evolving, so do the stones. The
royal azel has not as yet attained
its full vibrational capabilities
in relation to healing.

ROYAL AZEL: EARTH sign.

RUBY

The ruby has the fire of the universe.

When a person has tremendous compassion and wears the ruby, it intensifies that compassion. However, if that person is also working with ego, the ruby will be too intensifying and it's going to be the ego that takes the energy, not the compassion.

Wear the ruby on your left hand. It will enhance your life style.

If you pick up a ruby and get a feeling of strength from it, never superior to another, but an inner strength, then wear it.

If you have a temper, don't wear the ruby or the color red.

Be careful of the ruby, because it does have so much energy.

If the WATER sign would get a ruby, and wear it on the left hand, it would balance them so that they become more attuned to the universe, to their own body, and they would begin to realize how beautiful and unique they are.

RUBY: FIRE sign.

BLUE SAPPHIRE

When someone is extremely frustrated, the blue sapphire can stabilize
them.

This stone helps one flow to the
ultimate fulfillment.

The blue sapphire helps the blood
flow in a less constrictive manner.

The thyroid and heart also receive
a more flowing force from this
stone.

BLUE SAPPHIRE: AIR sign.

BLUE STAR SAPPHIRE

The star sapphire incorporates more than one thing.

The blue creates the balance; the wisdom; the stabilization. It also has the white and that white is the spiritual wisdom.

When someone wears a star sapphire, you're going to see an inner, loving rebellion. They'll begin to speak more and with a great deal of inner wisdom.

The star sapphire will totally change their vibration.

STAR SAPPHIRE: AIR sign (light)

EARTH sign (dense)

SERPENTINE

The natural serpentine is a pale green shade.

It promotes a gradual healing process within the body.

Serpentine is similar to the white onyx, but not as powerful.

This is a beautiful gentle stone that will benefit any wearer.

BLACK SERPENTINE

This has the same qualities as the black onyx.

SERPENTINE: EARTH sign (dense).

AIR sign (light).

SMOKEY QUARTZ

This is a quartz crystal with a smokey appearance.

The stone is connected with ultra sound - the sounds of the universe.

The smokey quartz will create a fine tuning in the ears and you'll become more aware of sounds.

You probably won't hear voices, but it will help you pick up thought forms, telepathic messages.

The smokey quartz also works to stabilize the heart.

SMOKEY QUARTZ: AIR sign.

SODALITE

Often mistaken for lapis, the
sodalite is a darker shade of blue
and may have some white flecks in
it.

This is a stone that can be worn by
anyone who needs to speak more and
gain more confidence.

With the sodalite, and the blue
onyx, we are dealing with all the
benefits of the color blue -
flowing, communicating, and serenity.

If you're upset or nervous, use
blue. It will calm you.

The sodalite also stabilizes the
thyroid area. This is extremely
important because the thyroid is a
gland in the throat area which
regulates the balance of the body,

cell and nerve growth. It is the metabolic rate that is affected by the thyroid.

Wear the sodalite at the throat area.

SODALITE: EARTH sign.

TIGER EYE

It's a tremendous stabilizer and works best when someone has started to become more spiritual.

The tiger eye works in a manner similar to silver.

Although it seems more suitable to a gold setting, if you put it in silver, you'll find that the stabilization is far greater than anticipated.

The tiger eye picks up the sounds of the earth, the pulsation. We need that balance to appreciate the earth before we can fully appreciate ourselves. It is important to know that we are a "part of" the earth, not "apart from" it.

RED TIGER EYE

Red is the color of the fire and
energy. With the red tiger eye, it
enhances one's ability to grow
toward a greater self-fulfillment.

TIGER EYE: EARTH sign.

: **TOPAZ**

If you want to conquer your fears, wear a topaz.

Worn as a ring or a necklace, the sun's rays can easily revitalize it and one day, you'll discover all your fears have vanished.

If you're defensive or have fears of rejection, the topaz will help to eliminate that too.

SMOKEY TOPAZ

Another stone that is attuned to the universal sounds and makes you more of a "receiver" of thought forms or telepathic messages.

TOPAZ, SMOKEY TOPAZ: AIR sign.

TOURMALINE

This stone has a tremendous range of colors, but the most commonly seen are the varying tones of greens and pinks.

The tourmaline is attuned to the sounds of the universe. Wearing this stone, then, makes you more of a "receiver" (telepathic messages).

The tourmaline not only transmits the sounds of the universe, but the pulsations of the earth as well.

The tourmaline creates a greater awareness of <u>all</u> things to the "receiver".

TOURMALINE: AIR sign.

TURQUOISE

The turquoise is the green of the earth, the blue of the sky, and a bit of black for protection.

It creates a unit of balance between the earth, the universe, and self.

The turquoise enhances your need to fulfill yourself and gives the wearer more confidence.

It stabilizes the earth and the universal vibrations so you can proceed at a steady pace. Not too fast, but just right, as you develop your spiritual awareness.

Widely used by the Indians to make them balance physically and mentally to the rain, sun, and earth. The turquoise brings greater awareness

of all things necessary for the
progression of life within man and
animal.

TURQUOISE: EARTH sign.

C H A P T E R   VIII

HEALING

WITH COLORED CLOTHS

You are affected by the colors you wear; the colors around you.

Not too many years ago, every fabric was a synthetic. Look at your catalogues now. Chamois shirts, flannel sheets; all cotton or wool fabrics.

You can _heal_ using _all_ natural fabrics in various colors.

You have absolutely nothing to lose by trying the methods we're about to describe, and you have much to gain.

It _works_.

The cloth used for healing _must_ be of one hundred percent natural fiber.

You use it for at least ten minutes, _never_ more than fifteen. You can do the healing several times a day.

When you're through with the cloth, flick it several times with your wrist (just snap it in the air). If it's soiled, wash it. As you do with your gemstones, place the cloths in the sun so they can be revitalized.

So now we're telling you that you can heal with a red flannel cloth, but don't leave it on more than fifteen minutes. You surely must be curious about great grandfather Jones who wore red flannel long-johns every day.

The difference is - "intent".

Your "intent" when you wear an all cotton shirt with your blue jeans is not the same as your "intent" when you put an all cotton piece of cloth on an infected finger for ten minutes, knowing that all the universal forces will be working to promote the healing.

Always go to a meditative state when you do the healings.

There's very little to purchase. Look around your house. You probably have T-shirts in all cotton, flannel shirts, wool sweaters, and most towels are made of all natural fibers.

To heal, simply put the cloth on the area that hurts, get into a meditative state, but do be aware of the time. Fifteen minutes is the limit. After that length of time, if the cloth remains on the infected area, the color of the cloth will intensify the infection, because like attracts like.

BLUE CLOTH

Blue lets things flow. It will stabilize, cool and "unknot".

For a stomach, leg or shoulder cramp, caused by a muscle being "knotted" and not by an irritation, use a blue cloth.

With a blood clot, <u>don't use red</u>. Use blue, because it's cooler and will let things flow gently.

Varicose veins: Blue because it unclogs everything, lets it flow.

Sinus problems: Cobalt blue would be best. Place the cloth on your head. If you find there are times when this would be embarrassing, you can always go hide in a closet!

Tightened muscles: Blue for cooling and releasing.

GREEN CLOTH

Use a dark or a light shade, never a yellow/green.

Green is chlorophyll, the purifier of the blood, the life force of our trees. It rejuvenates the cells and renews the tissues.

If there's a lot of frustration in your life, which can certainly lead to heart problems, use a green cloth over the heart area once or twice a day. It will rejuvenate the cells and create a new strength.

To improve your eyesight, use a green cloth.

If you have any swelling, (water retention), use green on the area.

Arthritis pain - green will lower the pain factor and promote the healing.

When using any of the other color cloths for healing, you can always follow the procedure with a green cloth. Let's say you've used a red cloth to remove an irritation. Now the green cloth for ten minutes will help to promote the healing.

<u>RED CLOTH</u>

Like attracts like, so when there is an irritation, using a red cloth will draw out that irritation.

Bronchitis - use red, it's an infection to be drawn out.

Infection - red.

Tumor, abscess, inflammation - red.

WHITE CLOTH

The white will stabilize the nerve endings to a great degree and decrease the pain you're experiencing.

Use a white cloth for:

Hearing loss.

Nervous or tension headaches. Put on pain areas, and don't forget the back of the neck.

Allergies. Place cloth on the head (back to the closet).

YELLOW CLOTH

Use the yellow cloth for:
   spleen, pancreas, gall bladder.

When you have an infection that has
a yellowish or greenish cast or is
oozing yellow, be it an eye infection or a cut, use the yellow cloth
because like attracts like and it
will draw out the infection.

Follow up with a green cloth to
rejuvenate the tissues.

C H A P T E R   IX

USING

COLORED DRINKING GLASSES

FOR HEALING AND BALANCING

We're using the natural elements again. The sun. Water. Color. And from the earth, glass.

Put some water in a glass (not plastic) and leave it in the sun for a minimum of ten minutes. There's no special time. You can leave it in the sun for an hour, if you choose. As with the gemstones and cloths, this can be accomplished indoors.

The sun infiltrates the glass of water. You're consuming the ultra-violet rays to create a greater radiation within your cell struc-ture. It's a balancing and healing process for the body.

If you drank water from each of the glasses every day, it would be similar to taking a multi-vitamin. You'd be getting minute doses of zinc, cobalt, permanganate, copper, etc.

If you don't drink all of the water, put a cover on the glass and refrigerate until needed.

BLUE GLASS

The blue glass attracts minute particles of cobalt from the atmosphere, which creates a balance within the body.

Blue is the fifth energy center, communication, flowing, serenity, etc.

If you are angry, frustrated, or have a lot of nervous energy, drink some water from the blue glass. Within minutes, you'll be much calmer.

A great aid to dieting when you're so hungry you could eat the wood-work.

Works as well as a tranquilizer.

Less habit forming than a sleeping pill.

GREEN GLASS

The green glass attracts the copper
from the universe.

Green is the color of the fourth
energy center - the heart.

Drinking the water from a green
glass will stabilize the emotions
of the heart area.

PURPLE GLASS

A purple glass will attract zinc
and cobalt as well as permanganate.

Drinking the water from the purple
glass will help to raise your
consciousness.

RED GLASS

The red glass attracts minute amounts of cadmium from the universe. Cadmium in large amounts is poisonous to our bodies, but in minute amounts, filtered from the universe, it will blend and energize the body.

If you're feeling "down", or need energy, drink the water from the red glass.

YELLOW GLASS

The yellow glass will attract
minute doses of sulfur from the
air.

If you're prone to kidney stones,
drinking the water from the yellow
glass will deter the formation of
the kidney stones.

It helps the sluggishness of the
liver. It is a kidney purifier.

C H A P T E R   X

THE

HEALING AND PROTECTIVE

LIGHTS

BLUE LIGHT

There is <u>no self-healing</u> which works as effectively as the blue light.

Sit in a meditative state and visualize the blue light entering through the crown energy center, and bathing the injured or painful area with a vibrant blue color.

We know the double terminated crystal can reverse polarity to promote a healing. Bringing in the blue light <u>works faster</u> than the crystal for self-healing because you are reaching to the ultimate source, the universe, drawing it to you rather than bringing it through another object (the crystal).

The blue is the flowing process of the universe. This force is the most direct, the most clear.

You can use the blue light every day during meditation for self-healing and for maintaining good health.

You cannot send this blue light to anyone else for their healing. This energy can only be brought in through self. It is self-motivated, self-healing.

When you channel a healing to someone, suggest they use the blue light daily to further promote the healing.

If you're tense or frustrated, bring in the blue light. It will calm you.

GREEN LIGHT

Bring in the green light for the heart area, which is the fourth energy center.

Green is soothing.

Green is growth.

The green light can bring you beyond emotional stress.

ORANGE LIGHT

Orange is the color of the second energy center.

Bringing in the orange light diminishes urges of desire, but also adds energy; the same as the orange/brown gemstones.

PINK LIGHT

The pink light allows a person to stabilize the first and second energy centers.

Pink, therefore, strengthens the security area (root or base of the spine), and gives stability to the second energy center (the sensual), thus helping to eliminate the ego and bringing in more of a love vibration.

Send pink light when you want to improve a relationship with someone, perhaps a co-worker or an employee/ employer, whose vibration does not blend too well with yours. Whenever you see that person, mentally surround them with the pink light. Anytime you think or speak of them, visualize the pink light all around them.

Pink is love and that's the vibration you're sending out. But it's a
two-fold gift. When you're sending
pink light, you're no longer feeling
animosity. Since everything we think
or feel is reflected in our electro-
magnetic field, others "sense" our
antagonism.

Sending pink light will alter the
entire relationship.

Remember, whenever you're frustrated
or angry with someone, you're not
"flowing". Use the pink light.

Everyday, when you meditate, you
might send pink light to every
consciousness everywhere.

It's a beautiful gift to the
universe.

PURPLE LIGHT

When you're not feeling very "spiritual"; when someone has irritated you or you feel your ego is getting in the way, you can bring in the purple light and gain a bit of spiritual wisdom.

If you feel a craving or fear, bring in the purple light.

You do not send purple light to someone else. When one begins their spiritual growth, you cannot bombard them with too much purple. They have a right to go along at their own pace.

<u>RED LIGHT</u>

When you're in need of energy,
bring in the red light.

WHITE LIGHT

The white light is the ultimate in purity and protection.

Bring in the white light when you're doing a quick "centering" or in meditation. It feels wonderful because white is total transformation.

When you're driving, instead of becoming angry at a driver who cut in front of you without signaling, surround that driver's car with white light. It will not only help to protect him, but other drivers as well (possibly from him).

Perhaps there's a storm, and you want to protect your home. Put white light around it. This does not mean to say that as the flood waters rise above your ankles, you stand there and say, "But I put white light around my house - it can't float away". It sure can! But the protective white light may have given you the opportunity to save a few possessions - including your life.

Dangerous road conditions (sleet, snow, wet leaves)--put white light around the car you're in.

For anything and everything you wish to protect, simply remember to bring in the universal energies through the white light. Surround yourself or an object - <u>bathe</u> it in the light.

During meditation, bring the white light in through the crown energy center and feel it expand throughout your being.

You will <u>feel</u> the transformation of the white light.

This book is simply a tool. Use it.
Maybe one day soon, you'll be
teaching a course based on it.

M.W.C.

ABOUT THE AUTHOR

An interest in the affects of colors
and gemstones led Marie and her hus-
band, Marty, to form their own company, *THE TRIAD*, specializing in mineral specimens, jewelry, and crystals.
The Triad participates in many of
the New Age fairs in New England.

Marie has appeared on cable TV and
has lectured throughout the area on
the attributes of gemstones and color.